Everything you need to know about
SNAKES
AND OTHER SCALY REPTILES

DK

Penguin
Random
House

Written by John Woodward
Consultant Dr. Kim Bryan

DK London
Editor Sam Priddy
Designer Hedi Hunter
Additional design Daniela Boraschi,
Richard Horsford, Fiona Macdonald
US Editors Shannon Beatty, John Searcy
Picture researcher Rob Nunn
Jacket designer Laura Brim
Producer, pre-production Rebekah Parsons-King
Senior producer Alice Sykes
Managing editor Julie Ferris
Managing art editor Owen Peyton Jones
Publisher Sarah Larter
Associate publishing director Liz Wheeler
Art director Phil Ormerod
Publishing director Jonathan Metcalf

DK Delhi
Senior editor Alka Ranjan
Senior designer Devika Dwarkadas
Editor Neha Pande
Designers Rakesh Khundongbam, Vaibhav Rastogi
Senior DTP designer Harish Aggarwal
DTP designers Arvind Kumar, Rajesh Singh
Managing editor Rohan Sinha
Managing art editor Sudakshina Basu
Production manager Pankaj Sharma
DTP manager Balwant Singh

First American Edition, 2013
Published in the United States by
DK Publishing,1450 Broadway,
Suite 801, New York, NY 10018

Published in Great Britain by Dorling Kindersley Limited.

A catalog record for this book is available from the
Library of Congress.

ISBN: 978-1-4654-0246-2

DK books are available at special discounts when purchased
in bulk for sales promotions, premiums, fund-raising, or
educational use. For details, contact: DK Publishing Special
Markets, 1450 Broadway, Suite 801, New York, NY 10018
or SpecialSales@dk.com.

Printed in China

For the curious

www.dk.com

Smithsonian Institution

This trademark is owned by the Smithsonian Institution and
is registered in the U.S. Patent and Trademark Office.

Consultant: Jeremy F. Jacobs is Collection Manager of
the National Museum of Natural History's Division of
Amphibians and Reptiles, Smithsonian Institution, USA.

Established in 1846, the Smithsonian Institution—the world's
largest museum and research complex—includes 19 museums
and galleries and the National Zoological Park. The total number
of objects, works of art, and specimens in the Smithsonian's
collection is estimated at 137 million. The Smithsonian is a
renowned research center, dedicated to public education, national
service, and scholarship in the arts, sciences, and history.

CONTENTS

Eyelash viper

Fire skink

Reptiles are a group of scaly, COLD-BLOODED creatures that includes *crocodiles, tortoises, lizards, and snakes.*

Big crocodiles have fearsome teeth and can eat you alive. Tortoises can live for more than *150 years.* Some **lizards** are the size of a fingernail; others are bigger than an adult man.

Aldabra giant tortoise

Slithering snakes are feared for their DEADLY VENOM. Yet most snakes are **not venomous** at all and many have beautiful colors and markings.

Nile crocodile

Reptile **family tree**

All reptiles are descended from the same ancestor that lived more than 300 million years ago. Very early in reptile history, a group split off and evolved into the turtles and tortoises. Later, one branch of the family tree produced the tuatara, lizards, and snakes, while another developed into the crocodilians, dinosaurs, and—perhaps surprisingly—birds.

Green iguana

LIZARDS

Lizards range from the giant Komodo dragon to tiny chameleons that could perch on your fingertip. In total, there are about 5,800 species, including iguanas, geckos, and skinks. Most lizards have four legs, but some don't have any and can be confused with snakes.

Tuatara

Gecko

TUATARA

There are only two living species of tuatara, both of which are found in New Zealand. They look a lot like lizards, but have a few different features. They are the only survivors of a group of reptiles that flourished during the age of dinosaurs, but most of them died out 100 million years ago.

Green sea turtle

Tortoises and **TURTLES**

Instantly recognizable by their shells, these reptiles have lived on the planet for at least 220 million years. In total, there are 327 different species. Tortoises are famously slow on their feet, but many turtles are agile, graceful swimmers.

Leopard tortoise

Most reptiles are **cold-blooded,**

SNAKES

These highly specialized reptiles evolved from a group of lizards just over 100 million years ago. Some—the pythons and boas—still have traces of back legs. There are about 3,400 species, all dedicated hunters that swallow their prey whole. Most are harmless, but some have a venomous bite that can be deadly.

BIRDS

The giant dinosaurs became extinct 65 million years ago, but one group of small, warm-blooded, feathered dinosaurs survived and evolved into birds. Although they are essentially living dinosaurs, birds are usually classified in a group of their own, separate from reptiles.

Macaw

Pit viper

Cryolophosaurus

Tree boa

American alligator

DINOSAURS

Closely related to crocodilians, dinosaurs appeared about 230 million years ago and evolved into the most amazing land animals that have ever existed. Some were huge, lumbering plant-eaters, while others were fast, agile hunters that were probably warm-blooded, unlike typical reptiles.

CROCODILIANS

The largest and most ferocious of all living reptiles, the crocodilians consist of crocodiles, alligators, caimans, and the long-snouted gharial. They have an ancient history dating back to before the dinosaurs, but today there are just 25 living species.

have **scaly skin**, and **lay eggs**.

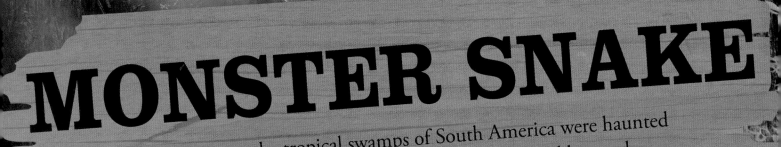

MONSTER SNAKE

Sixty million years ago, the tropical swamps of South America were haunted by one of the biggest snakes that ever lived. As long as a school bus and weighing more than 20 people, *Titanoboa* was a colossal constrictor that would have eaten crocodiles for breakfast.

Discovery

Scientists discovered fossils of *Titanoboa* in a coal mine in Colombia. The bones were so big that at first the scientists thought they were the remains of crocodiles. But soon they realized they were looking at the bones of a giant snake.

Titanoboa vertebra compared to that of a modern boa.

What it ate   *Blunt-nosed crocodile*

Titanoboa's bones show that it was related to the modern boa constrictor. It probably hunted in the same way, using its powerful body to squeeze the life out of its victims. *Titanoboa* preyed on crocodiles and giant tortoises.

Coal turtle

Where it lived

Like the modern anaconda, this giant boa lived in flooded tropical rainforests. All the biggest snakes alive today live in hot climates, and *Titanoboa*'s epic size means that the climate must have been even hotter then.

Robotic Titanoboa

A team of expert engineers in Canada has built a robotic, life-size version of *Titanoboa* to study how it moved.

Robotic **Titanoboa**

Snakes fact file

Snakes are reptiles with long, legless bodies that are covered in scales. These scales can be rough or smooth, and come in lots of colors and patterns. There are about 3,600 different types of snakes in the world, and most of them live in tropical habitats.

TEXAS THREAD SNAKE

Length: 6–11 in (15–27 cm)

Habitat: Dry and desert areas

Diet: Termites and other small insects

This tiny snake from the American desert is often mistaken for a worm, as it is pink and lives in soil. Its eyes are covered in scales since it doesn't need to see underground.

Scale

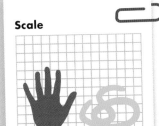

This snake has smooth scales and a short tail.

A cobra spreads its hood to make it look bigger.

KING COBRA

Scale

Length: 10 ft (3–4 m)

Habitat: Forests

Diet: Other snakes

The king cobra is the longest venomous snake in the world. It can raise up to two-thirds of its body off the ground, and spreads its hood wide if it feels threatened.

Spots help this snake to blend in against plants.

The world's **heaviest** snake, **the anaconda**, can weigh up to **500 lb (227 kg)**.

Scale

ROYAL PYTHON

Length: 3–5 ft (1–1.5 m)

Habitat: Grasslands and dry forests

Diet: Birds and small mammals

This West African snake is also known as the ball python because it rolls itself up into a ball when it gets scared. It is a constrictor, which means it squeezes its prey to death.

PARADISE TREE SNAKE

Length: Up to 3 ft (0.9 m)

Habitat: Tropical forests

Diet: Lizards, frogs, bats, and birds

This snake from tropical Asia can glide through the air for up to 328 ft (100 m) by making its body flat like a wing.

Scale

This snake has a row of red spots that runs down its back.

Snake babies

Like other typical reptiles, most snakes lay eggs. They generally lay them in warm places and leave them there, so when the young snakes hatch they have to find their own way in the world. However, baby snakes are able to take care of themselves, and newly hatched venomous snakes are just as dangerous as their parents.

1

Egg

Snake eggs have flexible, leathery skins instead of brittle shells like those of bird eggs. In general, the bigger the female snake, the more eggs she lays. Some pythons may lay more than 100 eggs at a time.

2

Incubation

Snakes must lay their eggs in warm places or they will not develop. Many, such as this grass snake, use heaps of vegetation that warm up as they decay. Some snakes guard their eggs by coiling around them, and a few pythons generate heat to keep them warm.

Live young

Although most snakes lay eggs, some give birth to live young. These include boas, most sea snakes, and many vipers, such as this European adder. The adder has up to 20 young at a time. Snake babies are independent soon after they are born and never stay with their mother for more than a few days.

3

Hatching

As a baby snake develops in its egg, it eventually needs extra oxygen and this makes it attempt to hatch. It cuts through the leathery shell with the sharp egg-tooth on its snout and takes its first look at the world.

4

Baby snake

It can be several hours before a hatchling snake slips out of its egg. The babies are cautious, and for good reason— even venomous baby snakes have a lot of enemies. But they usually leave the nest within a few days.

A SNAKE'S SKIN is studded with **hard scales** made of keratin—the same material as your **fingernails**. The *skin* and *scales* are **stretchy** and **tough**, but over time they get damaged. The snake SHEDS the *damaged outer layer* of skin to reveal a **shiny new one**.

The color cells in the skin lie below a transparent outer layer. This means the pattern of a snake, such as this **gaboon viper**, is not lost when it sheds its skin. It just gets brighter.

SCALY SKIN

Textures and patterns

Different snakes have different types of scales. Some are smooth, some are bumpy, and some have ridges down the center. Scales may form a flat sheet, especially on the head, or overlap at the back like roof tiles. Scales also contain color cells that give the snake its pattern.

Leaf viper

The **Asian file snake** lives in water and kills its prey by constriction. Its scales have a **rough texture** to give the snake a good grip on its victims.

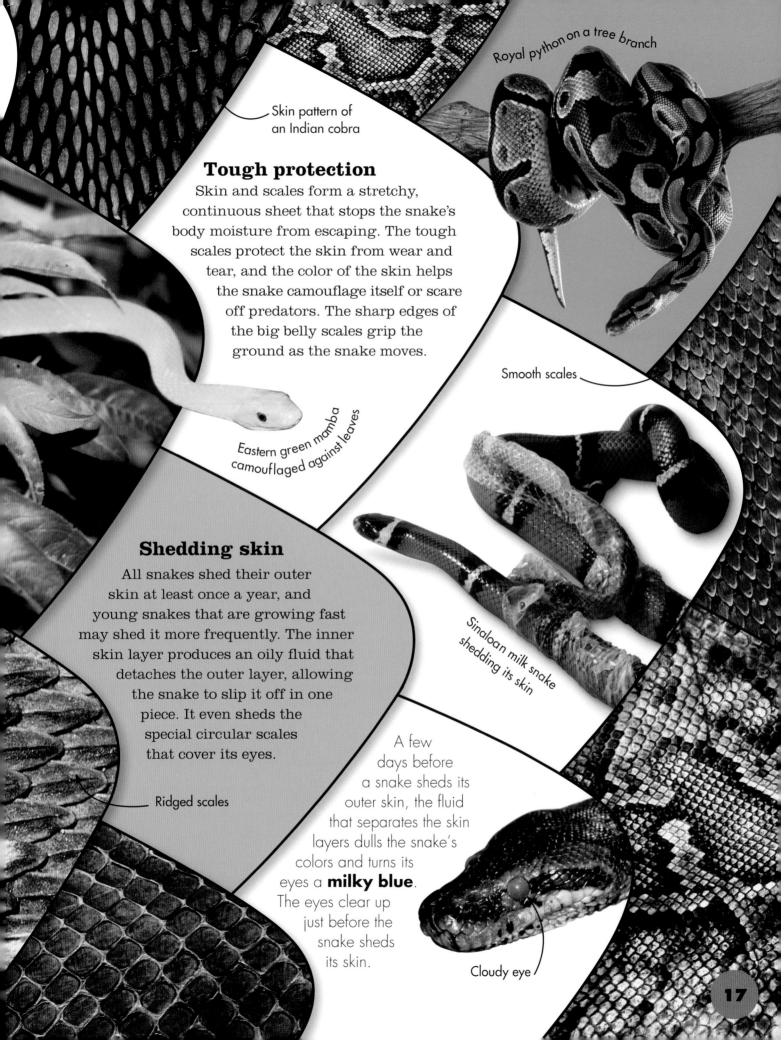

Skin pattern of an Indian cobra

Tough protection

Skin and scales form a stretchy, continuous sheet that stops the snake's body moisture from escaping. The tough scales protect the skin from wear and tear, and the color of the skin helps the snake camouflage itself or scare off predators. The sharp edges of the big belly scales grip the ground as the snake moves.

Royal python on a tree branch

Eastern green mamba camouflaged against leaves

Smooth scales

Shedding skin

All snakes shed their outer skin at least once a year, and young snakes that are growing fast may shed it more frequently. The inner skin layer produces an oily fluid that detaches the outer layer, allowing the snake to slip it off in one piece. It even sheds the special circular scales that cover its eyes.

Sinaloan milk snake shedding its skin

Ridged scales

A few days before a snake sheds its outer skin, the fluid that separates the skin layers dulls the snake's colors and turns its eyes a **milky blue**. The eyes clear up just before the snake sheds its skin.

Cloudy eye

17

HIBERNATION

Snakes can't cope with the **cold**. Unlike warm-blooded animals, they have no way of KEEPING WARM except for **basking** in the sunshine. If the temperature falls, the snakes will *cool down* with it. If it sinks **below 50°F (10°C)**, their bodies DON'T WORK PROPERLY. Therefore, snakes that live in regions with **cold winters** have to *hide away* in safe places **until spring**, often deep below the ground.

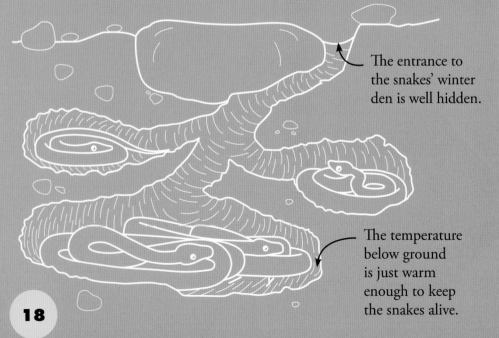

The entrance to the snakes' winter den is well hidden.

The temperature below ground is just warm enough to keep the snakes alive.

Wake-up time
American red-sided garter snakes hibernate in communal underground dens to survive the cold winters. In Canada, some dens contain thousands of these snakes, and they all emerge together into the spring sunlight in May.

DANCING ADDERS

As soon as a male European adder emerges from hibernation, he tries to find a female. He tracks her by picking up her scent trail.

Using his forked tongue to gather scent particles, another male is on the track of the same female. She is bigger than either of them, with browner skin.

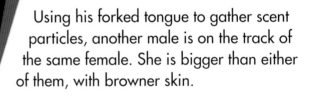

Both males catch up with the female at almost the same time, and there is trouble. The rivals fight for dominance by entwining their long bodies and wrestling with each other.

They lift their bodies off the ground, and twist and roll around in a ritual combat. They avoid doing any serious damage, and never bite each other.

As they match each other move for move, the writhing snakes look as if they are dancing. The dance can go on for several minutes before one snake gives up the struggle.

While the loser slithers away, the victor goes in search of the female hiding nearby. They get together and start another dance—but this one is a mating ritual.

RATTLESNAKE

The rattlesnake is one of the most amazing creatures ever to have lived. It is a dedicated hunter equipped with special senses for tracking and targeting its prey, and is armed with a superefficient weapon—hinged fangs for striking its prey dead.

Western diamondback rattlesnake

Rattle

The snake shakes its rattle to scare off enemies. Located at the tip of the tail, it is made of loose rings of hard, dry skin. A new ring is added to the rattle every time the snake sheds its skin.

Hinged fangs

The rattlesnake's extra-long fangs fold flat when it closes its mouth. Special bony structures push them forward when it opens its jaws wide to strike its prey.

Live bearer

Most snakes lay eggs in warm places, but rattlesnakes give birth to live babies. This allows them to live in cold climates where eggs might not stay warm enough to develop properly.

Expert hunter

The snake picks up the scent of prey with its flicking forked tongue, and targets it in the dark with its special heat sensors, located in pits under its eyes. With a quick stab, it injects a deadly dose of venom, then swallows the victim whole.

PROFILE

Species known

About 32

Most are called rattlesnakes, but the group also includes sidewinders.

Found in

North, Central, and South America—from southern Canada to Argentina.

Length

1–8 ft (0.3–2.5 m)

Pygmy rattlesnakes are among the smallest and eastern diamondbacks the largest.

Lifespan

20 years

Some rattlesnakes can live up to 20 years. However, many are killed by animals such as king snakes, which are immune to their venom.

SLITHERING snakes

Boa constrictor

RECTILINEAR Heavy snakes such as boas and pythons often creep forward on their bellies by raising parts of their bodies off the ground.

The snake pushes the lifted part of its body forward and lowers it so the big belly scales grip the ground. Then it lifts another part and does the same.

Green tree python

CONCERTINA When it is moving through tight spaces, the snake may grip the ground with the front half of its body and pull its tail forward.

Its body folds up in a series of tight loops, making it shorter. The snake then anchors the back part of its body, ready to push forward with the front.

Black mamba

SERPENTINE A snake such as the black mamba slithers along using curves of its long body to push against plants, stones, and earth.

As it wriggles, waves pass down its body from head to tail. Each curve is braced against an object, forcing the snake forward over the ground.

Sidewinder

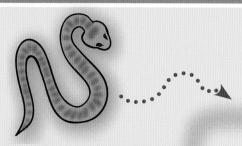

SIDEWINDING Some desert snakes use a special technique to move over soft, dry sand that would give way easily if they pushed against it.

The sidewinder throws the front part of its body sideways and plants it on the sand. A wave passing down its body lifts the back part so it follows the front.

Snakes move surprisingly well, considering they don't have legs. They can burrow, swim, and climb, as well as slither in a number of different ways. Some of these methods are faster than others. If these snakes were in a race, which one do you think would win?

The snake lifts several parts of its body at once, in waves that flow along its belly. They are not very obvious, so the snake seems to glide forward like a snail.

BURROWING Few snakes dig burrows, but many hunt or sleep in tunnels made by other animals. They move through them by using the concertina technique, bracing parts of their bodies against the burrow walls.

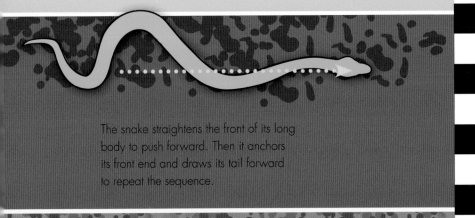

The snake straightens the front of its long body to push forward. Then it anchors its front end and draws its tail forward to repeat the sequence.

SWIMMING Snakes swim well, using the serpentine method to wriggle through the water like eels. It works because water is very dense, and resists being pushed against. Sea snakes have flattened tails that act like fins, improving efficiency.

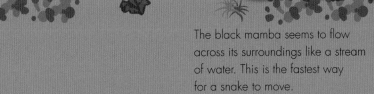

The black mamba seems to flow across its surroundings like a stream of water. This is the fastest way for a snake to move.

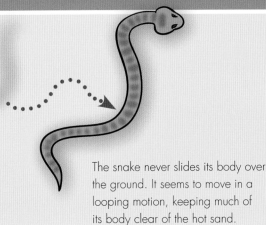

The snake never slides its body over the ground. It seems to move in a looping motion, keeping much of its body clear of the hot sand.

CLIMBING Tree-living snakes can use the serpentine technique to move through the branches in the same way that they flow through grass. But they can also employ the concertina method to climb up rough surfaces such as tree bark.

WHAT'S INSIDE?

Snakes evolved from lizards and have most of the same features, except for their legs. But they are very different inside—their skeletons and vital organs have been adapted and rearranged to suit their long snaky shape and allow them to swallow their prey in one huge mouthful.

Stomach
The snake's stomach is very stretchy to make room for big prey swallowed whole.

Liver
The largest organ in the snake's body, the liver removes toxic substances from its blood.

Glottis
This tube is an extension of the trachea, and allows the snake to breathe when its mouth is full.

Gullet
Powerful muscles in the wall of the gullet force the snake's prey down into its stomach.

Trachea
Rings of stiff cartilage keep the trachea open as the snake swallows its oversized meals.

The **green anaconda** is the world's

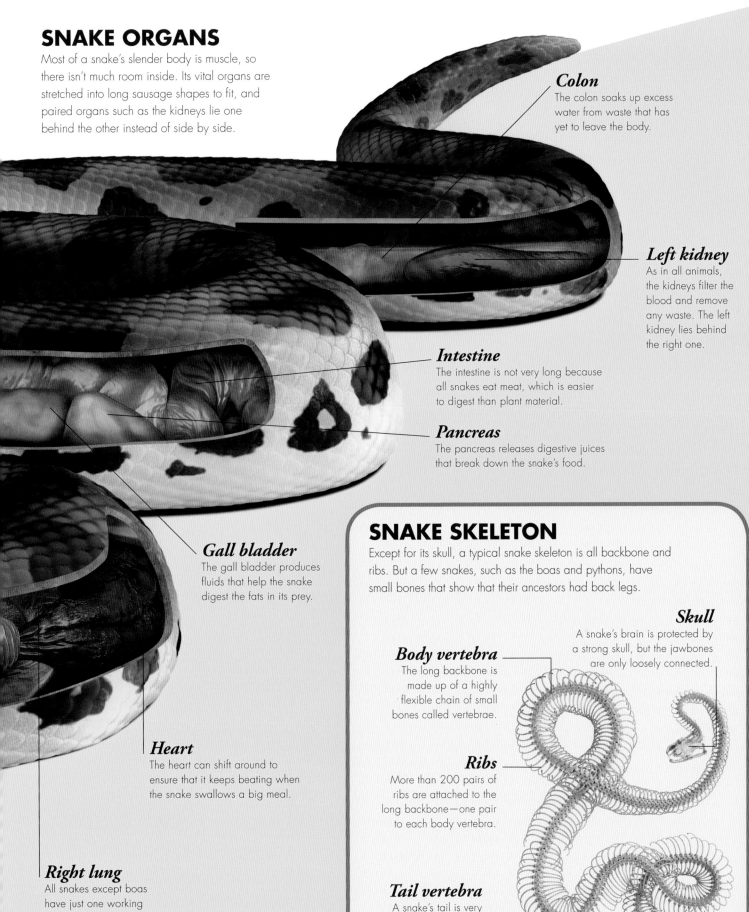

SNAKE ORGANS

Most of a snake's slender body is muscle, so there isn't much room inside. Its vital organs are stretched into long sausage shapes to fit, and paired organs such as the kidneys lie one behind the other instead of side by side.

Colon
The colon soaks up excess water from waste that has yet to leave the body.

Left kidney
As in all animals, the kidneys filter the blood and remove any waste. The left kidney lies behind the right one.

Intestine
The intestine is not very long because all snakes eat meat, which is easier to digest than plant material.

Pancreas
The pancreas releases digestive juices that break down the snake's food.

Gall bladder
The gall bladder produces fluids that help the snake digest the fats in its prey.

Heart
The heart can shift around to ensure that it keeps beating when the snake swallows a big meal.

Right lung
All snakes except boas have just one working lung. The left lung is tiny and doesn't do anything.

SNAKE SKELETON

Except for its skull, a typical snake skeleton is all backbone and ribs. But a few snakes, such as the boas and pythons, have small bones that show that their ancestors had back legs.

Skull
A snake's brain is protected by a strong skull, but the jawbones are only loosely connected.

Body vertebra
The long backbone is made up of a highly flexible chain of small bones called vertebrae.

Ribs
More than 200 pairs of ribs are attached to the long backbone—one pair to each body vertebra.

Tail vertebra
A snake's tail is very short, with far fewer vertebrae than its body. They don't have ribs attached to them.

heaviest snake.

Snake senses

Nearly all snakes are dedicated predators that need keen senses to locate their prey. But their senses are very different from ours, and some are almost impossible to imagine.

Touch

A snake can feel its way in the dark, thanks to special touch-sensitive scales on the head and other parts of its body. These allow the snake to sense the different textures of things such as sand, rocks, grass, moss, dry leaves, or tree bark.

See

Many snakes can see well, but only at close range. A snake's eyes have no eyelids, so it cannot blink or close them. Night hunters, such as this rattlesnake, have big pupils that close to slits during the day.

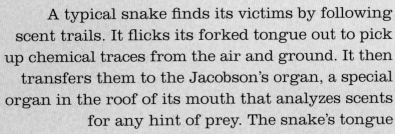

A typical snake finds its victims by following scent trails. It flicks its forked tongue out to pick up chemical traces from the air and ground. It then transfers them to the Jacobson's organ, a special organ in the roof of its mouth that analyzes scents for any hint of prey. The snake's tongue performs both smell and taste functions. This is why snakes are always flicking their tongues in and out.

Taste and smell

Hear

Snakes can't really hear sounds, because they have no proper ears. However, their jawbones are linked to sensors that pick up vibrations traveling through the ground. This makes them very sensitive to footsteps that might spell danger.

SUPER SENSE

Pit vipers, such as this rattlesnake, have pits under their eyes that contain infrared heat sensors. These allow them to "see" warm-blooded prey in total darkness and target them with deadly accuracy.

Rear-fanged
The boomslang's fangs are not hollow, but they are long and very sharp.

RATTLESNAKE
Found in the United States, the eastern diamondback rattlesnake is the largest species of rattlesnake and has a highly venomous bite. When in danger, it shakes a rattle on the end of its tail to scare off predators.

Long fangs
Exceptionally long fangs are used to inject venom deep into a victim's wound.

Scary fangs

BOOMSLANG
Most venomous snakes have long, hollow fangs that inject venom. But a "rear-fanged" snake like the boomslang has simpler ones near the back of its mouth that just bite into the victim, allowing toxic saliva to flow into the wounds.

Venomous snakes inject their victims

Hollow fangs
Fangs pump venom deep into the victim.

Venom gland
Venom is stored in venom glands at the back of the mouth.

Jawbone
In order to tackle larger prey, the jaw has to be able to open very wide.

Teeth
Small, sharp bottom teeth give the snake a tight grip on its prey.

PIT VIPER
Like all pit vipers, the two-striped forest pit viper has heat-detecting pits located in between its eyes and nostrils. It's responsible for many of the recorded snake bites in the Amazon rainforest.

Fang sheath
A viper's fangs are covered by fleshy sheaths when they aren't being used.

Baby snake
This baby pit viper's venom is as lethal as an adult's.

HOW FANGS WORK
When a rattlesnake is resting, its sharp fangs are folded back. When it gapes its mouth open, the fangs hinge forward, so the snake can use them to stab its victim. The muscles surrounding the venom glands then contract to squirt highly toxic venom through the fangs. The venom targets blood and internal organs, causing intense pain and vomiting.

Wide jaws
A stretchy lower jaw allows the snake to easily swallow prey as large as a rabbit.

puncture flesh before channeling *venom into the* prey.

BLACK MAMBA
This relative of the cobras has shorter fangs than a rattlesnake or viper, but they are just as effective. It's probably the deadliest species on the planet.

Dark threat
The black mamba gets its name from the color of the inside of its mouth.

using fangs—*special teeth designed to*

VENOM
Scientists "milk" snakes for their venom, which is then injected into a sheep to collect antibodies created by the sheep's immune system. These are used to create antivenoms to combat the effects of a snakebite. These usually work extremely well, provided the victim gets treated quickly enough.

Venom canal
Venom is channeled along enclosed grooves on the fangs and into the victim.

PUFF ADDER
Found in the rocky grasslands of Africa, this species of viper is usually active at night, when it ambushes unsuspecting prey.

VEN◆M

BOOMSLANG
Equipped with fangs in the rear of its mouth, this African tree snake has a powerful venom that stops its victim's blood from clotting, so it bleeds to death.

RATTLESNAKE
A rattlesnake is a type of viper, with a hemotoxic venom that causes massive bleeding and destroys flesh. It slows the blood circulation, causing the symptoms of shock.

SEA SNAKE
A sea snake needs extremely potent venom to stop its prey from escaping. It is myotoxic, paralyzing the victim's muscles. Luckily, sea snakes rarely bite.

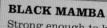

BLACK MAMBA
Strong enough to kill an elephant, black mamba venom attacks the nervous system and heart muscle with rapid, deadly effect.

Snake venom is a nightmare cocktail of poisons that might have been cooked up by a mad scientist. It is basically saliva, laced with powerful digestive juices that break down the tissues of the snake's prey. In the most venomous snakes, the mixture has been refined into a lethal weapon, used for both hunting and defense.

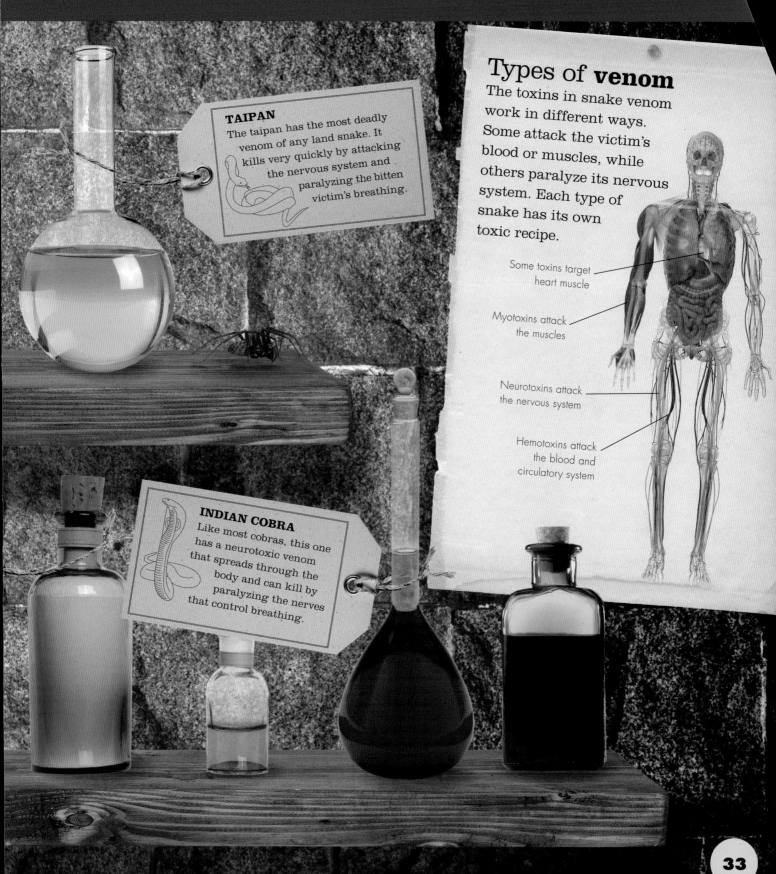

TAIPAN
The taipan has the most deadly venom of any land snake. It kills very quickly by attacking the nervous system and paralyzing the bitten victim's breathing.

Types of **venom**

The toxins in snake venom work in different ways. Some attack the victim's blood or muscles, while others paralyze its nervous system. Each type of snake has its own toxic recipe.

Some toxins target heart muscle

Myotoxins attack the muscles

Neurotoxins attack the nervous system

Hemotoxins attack the blood and circulatory system

INDIAN COBRA
Like most cobras, this one has a neurotoxic venom that spreads through the body and can kill by paralyzing the nerves that control breathing.

PITTING COBRA

Venomous snakes use their venom for hunting, but this toxic fluid also makes a potent defensive weapon. Most snakes have to strike at their enemies to use it, but spitting cobras can keep their distance and still defend themselves.

THREAT POSTURE

Venom is a precious resource, so a spitting cobra tries not to waste it. If threatened, it rears up in a classic cobra threat posture, flattening its neck into a hood that most people and animals recognize as a warning sign. They usually back off—and so does the cobra.

A spitting cobra can spray

VENOM SPRAY

If the cobra's threat posture doesn't scare off its enemy, it takes aim and sprays two jets of venom from its specially modified fangs. The spray cannot kill, but if the venom hits the eyes, it can blind the target.

FANCY FANGS

A spitting cobra's long, hollow fangs are modified, so that when the cobra compresses its venom glands, the venom squirts forward through the air instead of downward.

This cross-section of a spitting cobra's fang shows how the venom canal curves forward at the end, to project the venom spray in that direction.

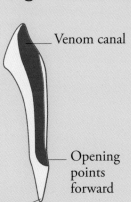

Venom canal

Opening points forward

Solid, sharp tip

The venom canal of a normal cobra fang has an elongated opening at the end that points straight down, to inject venom deep into its victim.

Venom enters fang here

Opening points down

MOST **DEADLY** SNAKES

Every year, up to 125,000 people die from snakebites. However, the most venomous snakes are not always the most dangerous, because many of them live in remote places where there are few people. The biggest killers live in densely populated countries where people are very likely to step on them, get bitten, and not receive proper treatment.

Australian taipan

The venom of this Australian snake is so toxic that its bites are deadly if not treated quickly. The closely related inland taipan, also found in Australia, is even more lethal. But both live in such remote regions that bites are rare.

Puff adder

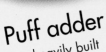

PRIME KILLER

This heavily built viper is the most dangerous snake in Africa. It gets its name from the way it puffs up its body and hisses in a threat display before striking with its very long fangs.

Gaboon viper

PRIME KILLER

Similar to the puff adder, this central African ambush killer has huge fangs that can be up to 2 in (5 cm) long—longer than those of any other snake.

Bushmaster

The South American bushmaster is the biggest of the pit vipers, growing to 10 ft (3 m) or more in length. Its venom can be fatal, but luckily bites are rare.

Desert death adder

Long fangs, big venom glands, and a very fast strike make this adder one of the deadliest snakes in Australia. However, since not many people live in its desert habitat, it claims very few victims.

Fer-de-lance

This highly venomous pit viper is the most deadly snake in South America. Many of its victims are bitten while working in banana plantations.

PRIME KILLER

Monocled cobra

Like all cobras, this South Asian snake tries to scare off its enemies with a threat display. But if that fails, it will bite, injecting a deadly venom.

PRIME KILLER

Saw-scaled viper

Its habit of lying near where people live means that this small Asian viper is often stepped on. As a result, it bites and kills thousands of people each year.

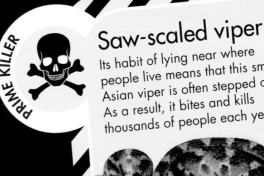

Tiger snake

The tiger snakes of southern Australia and Tasmania live in coastal regions and wetlands. Their venom is as deadly as that of a cobra.

Eastern brown snake

Its extremely toxic venom makes this the most dangerous Australian snake, but most of its victims recover if they are treated with antivenom in time.

37

A TIGHT SQUEEZE

The biggest snakes—pythons, *boas*, and the MIGHTY ANACONDA—don't need venom to kill their prey. They simply *coil* around their victims and use their MASSIVELY POWERFUL MUSCLES to **squeeze** the life out of them.

3. SQUEEZES

Every time its victim breathes out, the snake tightens its coils like a noose, so the animal cannot breathe in again. Before long, it goes limp due to lack of oxygen, and dies. But sometimes the relentless pressure stops its heart, killing it almost immediately.

2. STRIKES

Once the snake has a target in its sights, it moves fast, seizing the victim with its sharp teeth. These all curve backward, making it almost impossible for the prey to escape, no matter how much it struggles. With its prey secure, the snake loops its long body around it.

1. DETECTS PREY

As it glides along, the snake constantly samples the air with its flicking forked tongue, picking up scent particles. If it detects any trace of a possible victim, it tracks it like a bloodhound, searching for the strongest scent and following it until it reaches the source.

A constrictor doesn't **crush** its prey *to death*—it **throttles** *it.*

4. FINDS HEAD

Once the victim stops moving, the snake relaxes its grip and starts investigating with its tongue to see if it's edible. It must figure out which end is the head, because it has to swallow the meal headfirst or it will get stuck in its throat.

5. SWALLOWS

The snake opens its mouth wide and uses its mobile jaws to haul the prey slowly down its throat. Gradually, it engulfs the whole body.

A big python can easily subdue an ANTELOPE with its deadly **embrace.**

DIGESTS

If the snake swallows a really big victim, it ends up with a colossal bulge in its stomach. It can't move easily like this, so it usually slips into hiding where it can digest its meal in peace. This can take a week or more, as its powerful digestive juices break down skin, muscle, and even bone. And since a snake doesn't use much energy, a meal like this can keep it going for several months.

SWALLOWING PREY

Snakes are predators that kill and eat other animals. But unlike most hunters, they have no way of tearing their prey apart. Their sharp-pointed teeth are ideal for seizing and holding onto their victims, but not for slicing through skin and muscle. This means that they have to swallow their prey whole, in one big mouthful—and sometimes it can be very big indeed.

Viper's fangs hinge back

Teeth are sharp spikes

Glottis

The quadrate bone is attached to the jaw

Each side of the jaw is separate

Expandable jaws
A snake's lower jaw bones are hinged to quadrate bones that are themselves hinged to its skull, so the mouth can swing open incredibly wide. And since the lower jaw bones are not joined at the front, they can move apart to create an even larger gape.

Breathing space
With its mouth stuffed full of prey, a snake might struggle to breathe. But during swallowing, it opens its glottis (an extension of the trachea) at the very front of its mouth in order to gather vital air.

Full stretch

A python drags an antelope down its throat by moving one side of its lower jaw forward and getting a grip. It then moves the other side forward, before extending its upper jaw to engulf a little more. Once the food reaches the stomach, it's broken down by digestive juices.

A snake can swallow prey far bigger than its own head.

The gullet is muscular and stretchy

Crunch time

The egg-eating snake makes full use of its expandable jaws to swallow whole birds' eggs, eventually crushing them in its elastic gullet.

PYTHON VS. ALLIGATOR

The Burmese python and the American alligator are two of the most powerful reptiles on Earth. For thousands of years, they never met, but now in parts of America they live in the same swampy areas, compete for the same prey, and even eat each other. When they meet, there is always big trouble, but which one wins?

ROUND 5

Who will win? It's teeth and claws against coil upon coil of massively strong muscle.

American ALLIGATOR

Huge jaws and an armor-plated hide make the alligator almost invincible.

★★★★★ OVERALL SCORE

STRENGTHS

Powerful jaws

Big teeth

Sharp claws

Armored body

WEAKNESSES

Vulnerable to constriction

Can't swallow a python whole

Has to bite the snake's head

See the **struggle in the swamp** as

Location

The Florida Everglades in the southern United States are the natural home of American alligators. However, irresponsible owners have also released pet Burmese pythons into the area, and they're breeding. The alligators have been joined by hundreds—maybe thousands—of giant snakes.

SCORE

PYTHON 2
ALLIGATOR 2

Burmese PYTHON

A python can squeeze the breath out of an alligator, or even swallow it alive.

★ ★ ★ ★ **OVERALL SCORE**

STRENGTHS

Constricting coils

Very sharp teeth

Can swallow a small alligator whole

Fast and elusive

WEAKNESSES

Can't bite through armor

Can't escape if seized

Swallowing live prey can be fatal

Fighting Once an alligator gets its teeth into a python, it looks like it's all over. But unless the alligator bites into something vital, it won't kill the snake. It has to target the head. Meanwhile, the python can fight back by squeezing its coils around the alligator's body so it can't breathe. But if the snake swallows its enemy alive, the alligator's sharp claws could tear it apart from the inside!

two giant reptiles **fight to the death**.

SNAKE TALES

Many people are very scared of snakes—maybe with good reason. Snakes feature in many myths and legends, but they're not always the villains. Some tales even depict them as heroes, and in ancient Greek myths they were associated with medicine and healing.

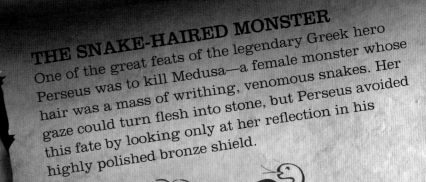

THE SNAKE-HAIRED MONSTER

One of the great feats of the legendary Greek hero Perseus was to kill Medusa—a female monster whose hair was a mass of writhing, venomous snakes. Her gaze could turn flesh into stone, but Perseus avoided this fate by looking only at her reflection in his highly polished bronze shield.

Thor and Jörmungandr

Medusa

THE LAST BATTLE

According to the Norse mythology of the Vikings, the world will come to an end in a battle known as the twilight of the gods. During the fight, a venomous serpent, Jörmungandr, will emerge from the ocean and poison the sky. The serpent will be killed by Thor, the god of thunder, but Thor himself will be poisoned by the serpent and fall dead.

TESHUB AND THE SERPENT

A Hittite myth from the Bronze Age tells the story of Teshub, the storm god, who was defeated by the giant snake Illuyanka. But Teshub's daughter Inara helped him get his revenge. She threw a great feast for Illuyanka, who ate so much that he couldn't get back into his hole, enabling Teshub to catch and kill him.

Illuyanka

KRISHNA AND VASUKI

According to Hindu mythology, soon after Lord Krishna was born, his father Vasudev tried to carry him across the Yamuna river to save him from his evil uncle, Kamsa. The river was in full flow and the water rose high over Vasudev's head. Vasuki, a huge cobra with several heads, rose above the raging waters and reared its hoods over the father and baby, before escorting them to the other side.

Vasudev carrying Krishna

Aido-Hwedo

THE COSMIC SERPENT

According to a west African legend, when the goddess Mawu created the Earth, it began to sink into the ocean. She asked the cosmic serpent Aido-Hwedo to coil around it and hold it up. Aido-Hwedo took the job, but would sometimes shift into a more comfortable position, causing an earthquake.

45

Snake or fake?

Snakes evolved from ancestors that had legs, but didn't use them. Some lizards have made the same evolutionary journey, and lost their legs too. They look a lot like snakes, but unlike them they have eyelids and proper ears. They also have normal lizard jaws, so they can't swallow big animals whole, and despite appearances they are all quite harmless.

Many lizards get by very well *without limbs*. Some LIVE UNDERGROUND, where legs would *just get in the way*. But others live just like **real snakes**.

WESTERN HOODED SCALY FOOT
HUNTS IN THE AUSTRALIAN DESERT.

SPECKLED WORM LIZARD
A BURROWER LIKE AN EARTHWORM.

CALIFORNIA LEGLESS LIZARD
LIVES IN AMERICAN SAND DUNES.

Cunning caterpillar
By pulling its head back into the front part of its body, the spicebush swallowtail caterpillar expands two big "eyespots" to make it look like a snake. It's a neat trick, because most insect-eating birds are scared of snakes. They take one look and back away quickly, leaving the caterpillar alone.

WANTED

REAL SNAKE

They might all look *guilty*, but **only one** of these snaky characters is a TRUE SNAKE.

SLOW WORM
A EUROPEAN LEGLESS LIZARD THAT LOVES EATING SLUGS.

COMMON SCALY FOOT
NAMED AFTER ITS TINY HIND LEGS.

ROUGH GREEN SNAKE
A NONVENOMOUS INSECT HUNTER.

Some reptiles have such amazing CAMOUFLAGE that they are almost *impossible to see*. Many rely on this to **hide from enemies**, but camouflaged snakes may also use their invisibility to **lie in ambush** for their prey. Here are some snakes and lizards hidden in their surroundings. *Can you spot them?*

HIDE and SEEK

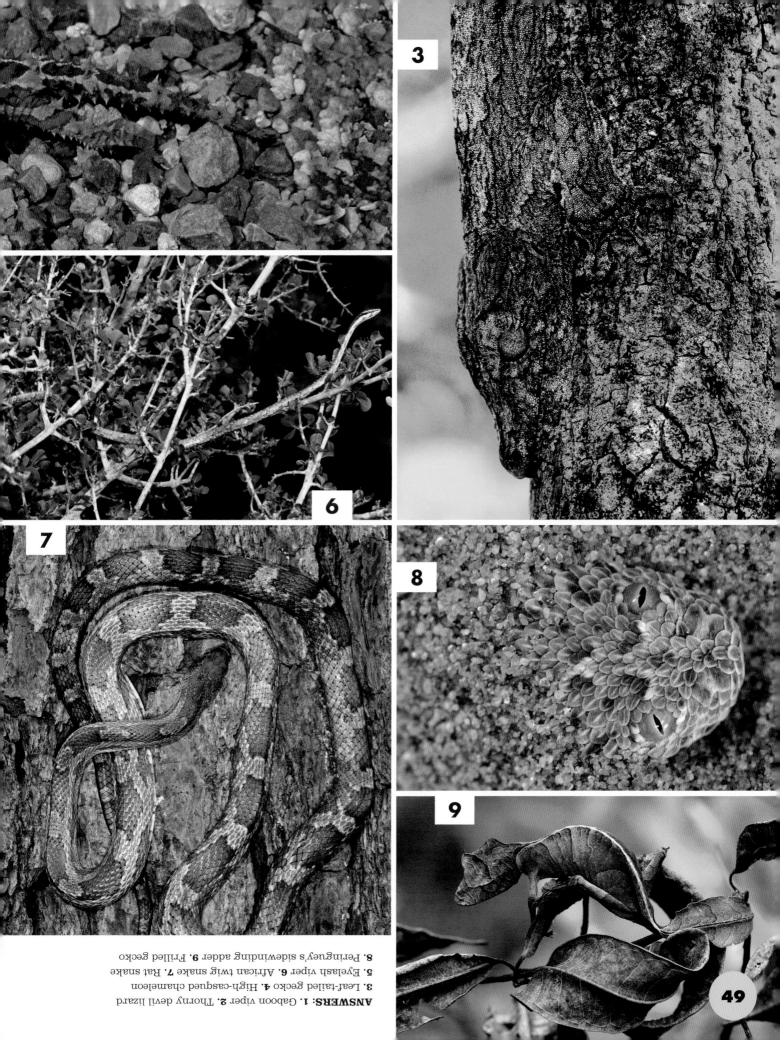

3

6

7

8

9

49

COLORFUL CHAMELEONS

Chameleons are known for their spooky eyes and long, sticky tongues. But they are most famous for being able to change their color at will, from dull brown or green to brilliant patterns of vivid red, blue, and yellow, right in front of your eyes.

SHOWING OFF

Most chameleons live in trees, where they stalk insects among the leaves. When relaxed, they are usually some shade of green, which helps to hide them from enemies such as birds. But if they get excited, they glow with vivid colors. Male chameleons use these to show off to rivals and maybe scare them away, or to attract females.

Panther chameleons are green…

but change color when they are

angry, happy, or sad.

KEEPING COOL

There's more to changing color than showing off. Dark colors soak up heat from the sun while pale colors reflect it, and chameleons can use this to control their body temperature. The Namaqua chameleon lives in the Namib Desert of Africa, where the nights are cold and the days are very hot. So it stays dark in the morning to absorb heat, then turns pale in the afternoon to avoid overheating.

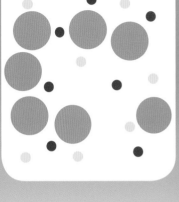

...and pale in the afternoon.

Namaqua chameleons are dark in the morning...

HOW DO CHAMELEONS CHANGE COLOR?

Chameleons have color cells in their skin called chromatophores. These are either red, yellow, blue, white, or black. The cells expand or contract to reveal or hide the colors—often changing the chameleon's skin color in less than a second.

When the red chromatophores expand and all the other color cells contract, the skin of the chameleon turns red.

If the red cells contract and the yellow ones expand instead, the chameleon's skin changes from red to yellow.

Expanded blue cells can turn the chameleon blue, and if the blue and yellow ones both expand, it turns green.

51

DEFENSE TACTICS

Small reptiles have many enemies. They include hawks and eagles, meat-eating mammals such as foxes, and other reptiles—especially snakes. Some reptiles have surprising ways of defending themselves by confusing, distracting, or even scaring their attackers into leaving them alone.

 PRICKLY BALL

 TAIL SNAPPER

Armadillo lizard
Many reptiles are armored with spiny scales. This African desert lizard turns itself into a prickly mouthful by curling up and gripping its own tail.

Moorish gecko
If attacked, most lizards have the ability to snap off their own tails. The tail thrashes around, distracting the attacker while the lizard makes its escape.

 FRILLED DISPLAY

Frilled lizard
If threatened, this big Australian lizard lunges forward and expands its enormous neck ruff, while hissing loudly with its mouth gaping open. It's enough to make most predators back off.

Grass snake

If all else fails, some snakes will flop on the ground with their tongues lolling and play dead. This works because most hunters prefer to eat freshly killed prey.

COLORFUL DODGER

Five-lined skink

Birds hunt by sight and notice bright colors. The vivid blue tail of this lizard distracts them from the lizard's vulnerable head.

RAISED HOOD

Monocled cobra

You might not think a cobra would have any enemies. But by rearing up and flattening its neck into its famous hood, this snake clearly lets any predators know what they are dealing with.

Little AND LARGE

Some REPTILES are real *monsters*. They include huge crocodiles, GIANT TORTOISES, and massively **powerful snakes**. But others are no bigger than the *flies* that buzz around the heads of their SUPERSIZED relatives.

ACTUAL SIZE

Micro **LIZARD**

This tiny chameleon (*Brookesia micra*) from Madagascar is one of the smallest known lizards—so small that it could perch on your fingertip. Nobody knew it existed until very recently. It hunts for insects among dead leaves on the forest floor by day, but climbs up into the trees at night.

Big brother
The colossal Aldabra giant tortoise weighs up to 794 lb (360 kg). That's more than 2,000 times as much as the tiny speckled padloper tortoise.

Long and strong
It takes four strong men to hold this green anaconda from the swamps of Amazonia. The biggest living snake, it can grow to at least 34 ft (10.4 m) long.

Island GIANT
At up to 11 ft (3.3 m) long, the Komodo dragon is the world's biggest lizard—a fearsome predator that can kill a buffalo and rip it to pieces with its sharp teeth. It lives on small islands near Java in Indonesia, where it preys mainly on deer, pigs, goats, and sometimes people.

What's for **dinner?**

Some reptiles are fearsome predators, while others prefer to munch on salad leaves. **Follow the colored lines to find these reptiles' favorite food.**

Emerald tree boa

This tree snake hunts by night in the Amazon rainforest, ambushing its furry prey from overhanging branches.

Grass and fruits

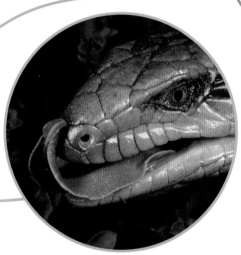

Blue-tongued skink

The weird blue tongue of this Australian lizard is useful for scooping up prey that doesn't sound very appetizing.

Praying mantises

Thorny devil

Named for its amazingly prickly skin, the Australian thorny devil has a taste for small biting insects.

Sea krait

This Southeast Asian sea snake uses highly toxic venom to hunt this slippery prey in the clear waters of coral seas.

Snails and dung beetles

Prairie dogs

Spur-thighed tortoise

Most animals could escape from this Mediterranean tortoise, so it eats things that won't run away.

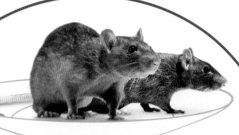

Rats

Jackson's chameleon

Peculiar swiveling eyes allow this east African chameleon to target these small, spiky insects with lethal accuracy.

Eel

Egg-eating snake

Unlike most of its kind, this African snake is not a true hunter, although many of the eggs that it eats contain developing baby birds.

Western diamondback rattlesnake

Like all rattlesnakes, this snake has heat sensors for detecting warm-bodied creatures that live in dark burrows.

Ants

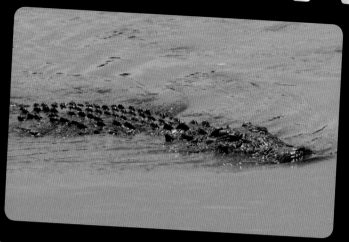

1 Massively powerful Nile crocodiles always hunt in the water. They watch and wait, then quietly sink below the surface to avoid scaring their prey too early.

Crocodile **ambush**

African Nile crocodiles are smart. They know when it's time for *migrating animals* to pass their way and cross the river, so they GATHER FOR A FEAST. As the animals take their first nervous steps into shallow water, the crocodiles lie low, then slowly slip into position for a ***devastating ambush***.

2 When prey, such as these wildebeests, start swimming, the crocodiles glide slowly toward them, often slipping underwater to take the animals by surprise.

3 Each crocodile picks out a likely victim. They usually target the stragglers, but this crocodile is hungry and ready to seize anything within range of its huge, terrifying jaws.

4 Suddenly, the killer bursts out of the water to grab its victim by the neck or snout. The crocodile drags the wildebeest underwater, holds it down until it drowns, then rips it apart.

WATER

Eastern garter snake
Equally at home on land and in the water, this snake is found in North America.

Reptiles have developed **different ways** of living in and around WATER and can be found in *ponds*, rivers, LAKES, and **oceans** the world over. Reptiles such as *sea turtles* are HIGHLY ADAPTED to marine environments and will only come onto *land* when they need to **lay their eggs**.

REPTILES

Green basilisk lizard
This Central American lizard has developed the ability to run short distances over water.

Other **reptiles** see water as the perfect **hunting ground**.

Anacondas will **drag** unsuspecting prey **underwater** before **constricting** them to *death*, while a *saltwater* crocodile managed to kill a **fully grown tiger** in 2011.

Saltwater crocodile
The largest reptile in the world, this crocodile has been spotted swimming in the open ocean.

Green turtle This large sea turtle grows up to 4.3 ft (1.3 m) long and is found in tropical oceans.

Sea *TURTLE* MIGRATION

Loggerhead sea turtles travel vast distances across the oceans to find food and breeding sites. In the north Pacific, they ride the ocean currents all the way from Japan to America and back, steering by Earth's magnetic field.

Off course
I've come too far north, and the sea is really cold. I just swam past an iceberg. I'll go south a bit to catch the ocean current that will carry me where I want to go. America, here I come!

ALEUTIAN
ISLANDS

ASIA

JAPAN

Hard work
I'm on the beach at Yakushima Island in Japan, but not for sunbathing. I've been up all night digging a hole for my eggs. I've just finished covering them with sand. Time for a long, cool swim!

BURIED EGGS

Although they are oceanic creatures, sea turtles must lay their eggs on land. They bury them in the sand of warm beaches on remote shores. When the baby turtles hatch, they dig themselves out, head for the open sea, and swim off into the blue.

Island paradise
The tropical current is carrying me west past these volcanic islands. The waves are huge! And what are these strange creatures riding them? Still some way to go before I reach Japan...

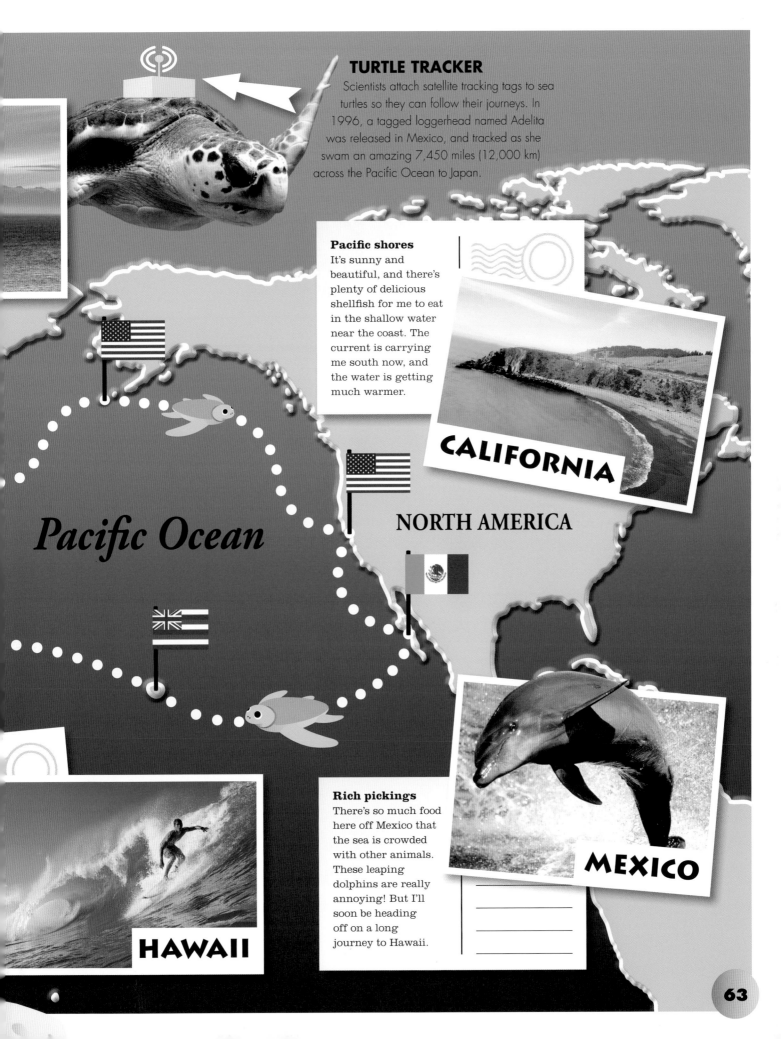

TURTLE TRACKER
Scientists attach satellite tracking tags to sea turtles so they can follow their journeys. In 1996, a tagged loggerhead named Adelita was released in Mexico, and tracked as she swam an amazing 7,450 miles (12,000 km) across the Pacific Ocean to Japan.

Pacific shores
It's sunny and beautiful, and there's plenty of delicious shellfish for me to eat in the shallow water near the coast. The current is carrying me south now, and the water is getting much warmer.

CALIFORNIA

Pacific Ocean

NORTH AMERICA

Rich pickings
There's so much food here off Mexico that the sea is crowded with other animals. These leaping dolphins are really annoying! But I'll soon be heading off on a long journey to Hawaii.

MEXICO

HAWAII

EXPERT CLIMBER

Geckos are small lizards that usually live in trees, but they often come into houses, where they scuttle up walls and glass windows and even cling upside down to ceilings. Their secret is the special pads on their toes, which seem to work almost like magnets.

GECKOS INSPIRE SCIENTISTS

Scientists at Stanford University in California have made Stickybot, a robot that can climb up glass like a real gecko. The key to the robot's success is its sticky toes that peel away from the glass the same way as those of a gecko.

Stickybot

Tokay gecko

Any dirt would stop the feet from gripping a surface, so a gecko's toe pads have a special self-cleaning mechanism.

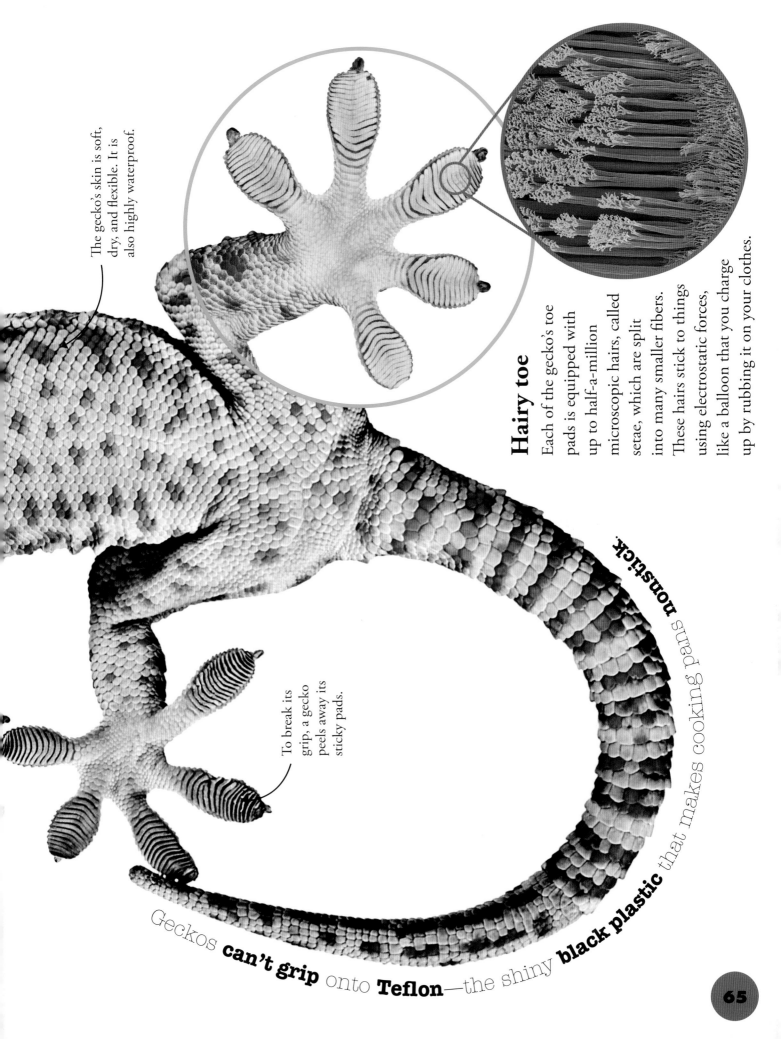

The gecko's skin is soft, dry, and flexible. It is also highly waterproof.

Hairy toe

Each of the gecko's toe pads is equipped with up to half-a-million microscopic hairs, called setae, which are split into many smaller fibers. These hairs stick to things using electrostatic forces, like a balloon that you charge up by rubbing it on your clothes.

To break its grip, a gecko peels away its sticky pads.

Geckos **can't grip** onto **Teflon**—the shiny **black plastic** that makes cooking pans **nonstick.**

Movie stars

Early filmmakers often used iguanas as monsters, because of their bizarre appearance. Space travelers in old movies landed on planets that were teeming with them. Iguanas were also used to play the part of dinosaurs—despite looking nothing like the real thing.

Light-sensing "third eye"

Planet of the IGUANAS

Many lizards look a little strange, but few are quite as weird as iguanas. They come in a dazzling variety of colors, and are adorned with long spines and oversized scales—especially the males. Add in a big flap of scaly skin beneath the throat, and iguanas look like visitors from another planet.

Extra eye

Iguanas have good hearing and excellent sight, with particularly good color vision. They can see more colors than we can, including ultraviolet. Green iguanas also have a "third eye" on top of their heads that detects light levels while they sleep.

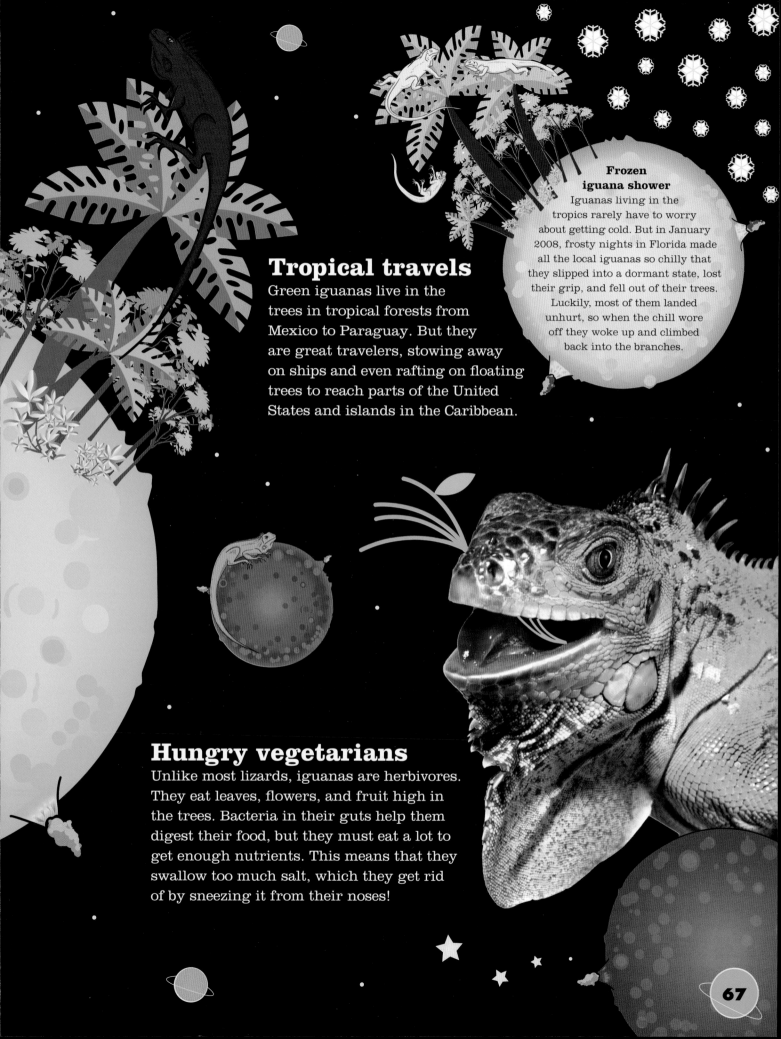

Tropical travels

Green iguanas live in the trees in tropical forests from Mexico to Paraguay. But they are great travelers, stowing away on ships and even rafting on floating trees to reach parts of the United States and islands in the Caribbean.

Frozen iguana shower
Iguanas living in the tropics rarely have to worry about getting cold. But in January 2008, frosty nights in Florida made all the local iguanas so chilly that they slipped into a dormant state, lost their grip, and fell out of their trees. Luckily, most of them landed unhurt, so when the chill wore off they woke up and climbed back into the branches.

Hungry vegetarians

Unlike most lizards, iguanas are herbivores. They eat leaves, flowers, and fruit high in the trees. Bacteria in their guts help them digest their food, but they must eat a lot to get enough nutrients. This means that they swallow too much salt, which they get rid of by sneezing it from their noses!

Living fossils

The tuataras of New Zealand may look like lizards, but they actually belong to a very different group of reptiles with just two living species. Most of the others became extinct long before the dinosaurs died out, so the last tuataras are like living fossils.

Homeosaurus

Pleurosaurus

Daily routine

Tuataras hide in burrows all day and only come out at night.

7:00 AM	sleeping
10:00 AM	sleeping
6:00 PM	still sleeping
11:00 PM	hunting

This is me

These are two of my distant ancestors

Relatives

We don't have any! Not now, at any rate. But 150 million years ago, we had plenty. Fossils of *Homeosaurus* and even the very slim, aquatic *Pleurosaurus* show that they were a lot like tuataras.

Ancient parents

A tuatara can live for an amazingly long time. One captive male named Henry was 114 years old in 2012, and he became a father for the first time at the age of 111.

This is my friend Henry. He is 114 years old!

Henry's babies

New Zealand

Map key
● Where to find tuataras

Where I live

Long ago, tuataras lived all over New Zealand. But people brought in other animals such as rats that ate our eggs, and now wild tuataras only live on rat-free islands just off the coast. But there are at least 60,000 of us!

Fame and fortune

Not surprisingly, tuataras are famous in New Zealand. The native Maori people saw them as spirits, and a tuatara once adorned the New Zealand five-cent coin. What a handsome guy!

DISGUSTING

The Komodo dragon is a *crocodile-sized* lizard that lives on a few SMALL ISLANDS near Java in Indonesia. It is a **killer**, but it's not PICKY and will eat ALMOST ANYTHING, however *disgusting*.

Dinnertime

An adult Komodo dragon can fell a fully grown deer with one blow of its powerful tail, then hold it down with its long claws while it uses its sharp, saw-blade teeth to rip it into bite-size mouthfuls.

DRAGONS

Cannibals

Big Komodo dragons are likely to eat smaller ones, so the younger dragons try to steer clear of the adults. They may also try to repel them by rolling in the revolting, half-digested gut contents of their prey.

Forked tongues

Komodo dragons are happy to eat the rotting remains of dead animals. Like other monitor lizards (and snakes), they have long forked tongues, which they use to sample the air for traces of food. They can pick up the smell of death from more than 6 miles (10 km) away.

NO CHILDREN ALLOWED!

To a Komodo dragon, a small human is just another tasty snack, so local people have to make sure that their children are not attacked and eaten.

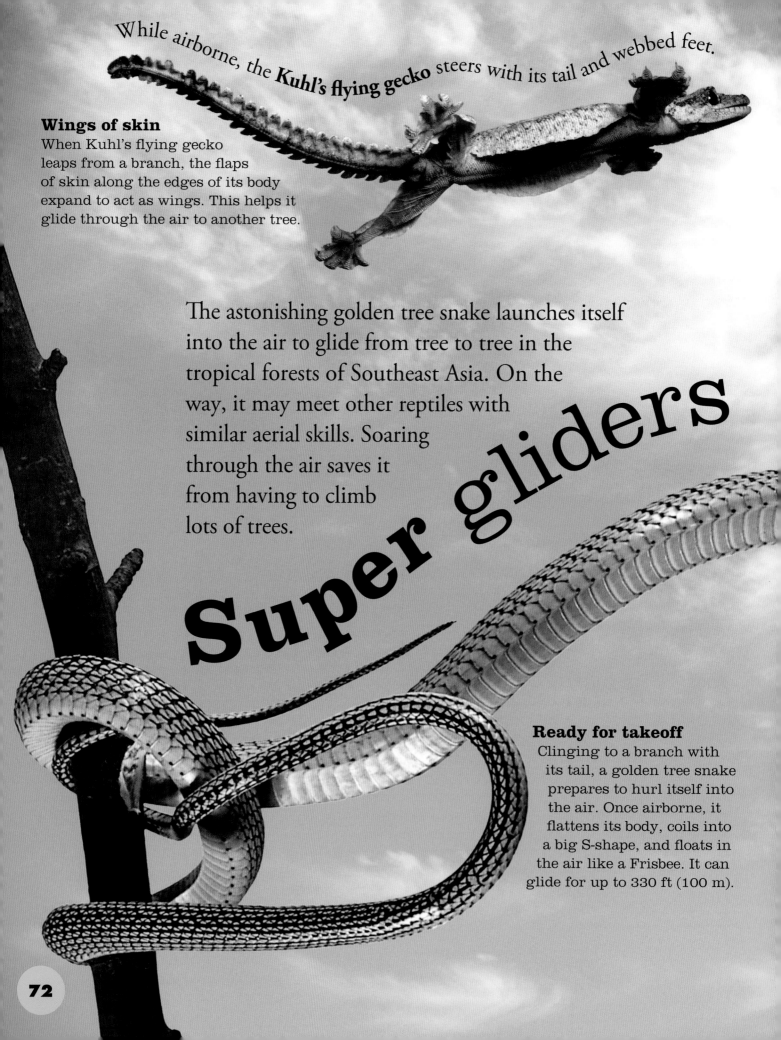

While airborne, the **Kuhl's flying gecko** steers with its tail and webbed feet.

Wings of skin
When Kuhl's flying gecko leaps from a branch, the flaps of skin along the edges of its body expand to act as wings. This helps it glide through the air to another tree.

The astonishing golden tree snake launches itself into the air to glide from tree to tree in the tropical forests of Southeast Asia. On the way, it may meet other reptiles with similar aerial skills. Soaring through the air saves it from having to climb lots of trees.

Super gliders

Ready for takeoff
Clinging to a branch with its tail, a golden tree snake prepares to hurl itself into the air. Once airborne, it flattens its body, coils into a big S-shape, and floats in the air like a Frisbee. It can glide for up to 330 ft (100 m).

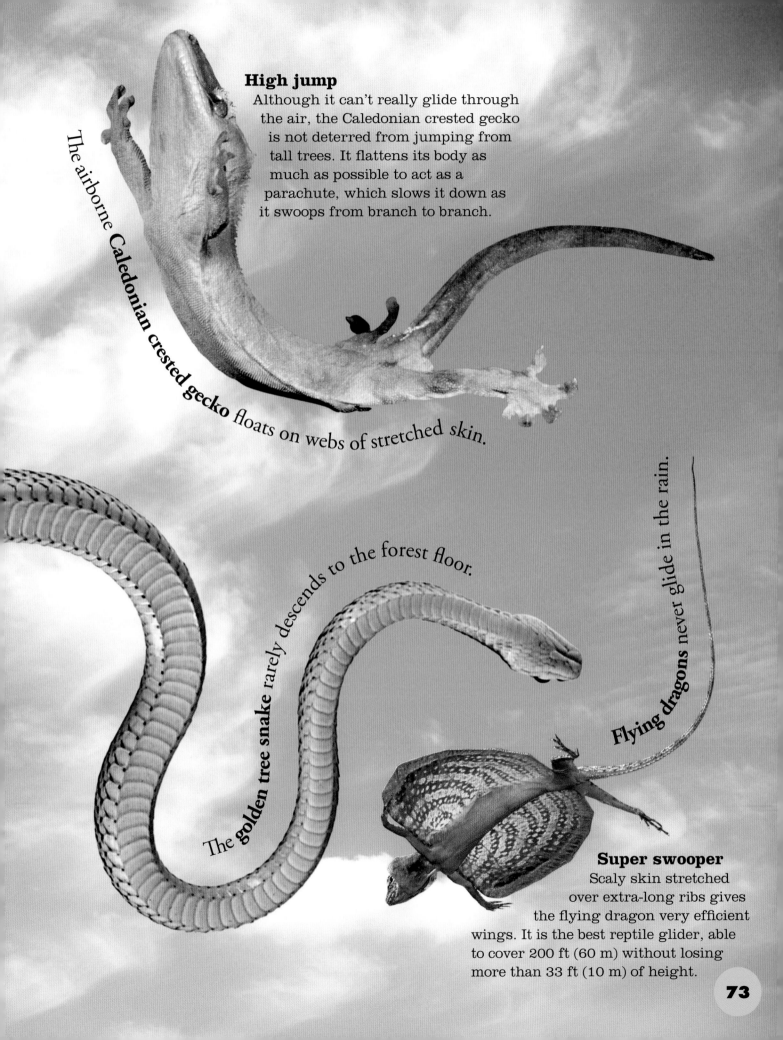

High jump

Although it can't really glide through the air, the Caledonian crested gecko is not deterred from jumping from tall trees. It flattens its body as much as possible to act as a parachute, which slows it down as it swoops from branch to branch.

The airborne Caledonian crested gecko floats on webs of stretched skin.

The golden tree snake rarely descends to the forest floor.

Flying dragons never glide in the rain.

Super swooper

Scaly skin stretched over extra-long ribs gives the flying dragon very efficient wings. It is the best reptile glider, able to cover 200 ft (60 m) without losing more than 33 ft (10 m) of height.

DESERT DWELLERS

Life is hard in the desert. It can be extremely hot, there's hardly any water, and very little to eat. But this suits reptiles. They can hide away in the heat of the day, their waterproof skins stop them from losing moisture, and they can survive on amazingly little food.

This chameleon can turn pale to reflect the desert sun.

Dancing lizard

Scorching hot desert sand can burn even a reptile's toes. When standing still, the African shovel-snouted lizard keeps itself cool by lifting two feet off the ground at once, then swapping to the other two feet in an elegant thermal dance.

Stilt walker

Most chameleons live in trees, but the Namaqua chameleon of the Namib Desert in Africa hunts insects on the ground. It uses an odd "stilt walk" to raise its body off the hot sand.

Sideways snake

Sidewinding is a perfect way for the Peringuey's sidewinding adder to move across the dry, soft sand dunes of the Namib Desert. It makes tracks in the sand as it throws its body forward. Its small size allows it to survive on very little food.

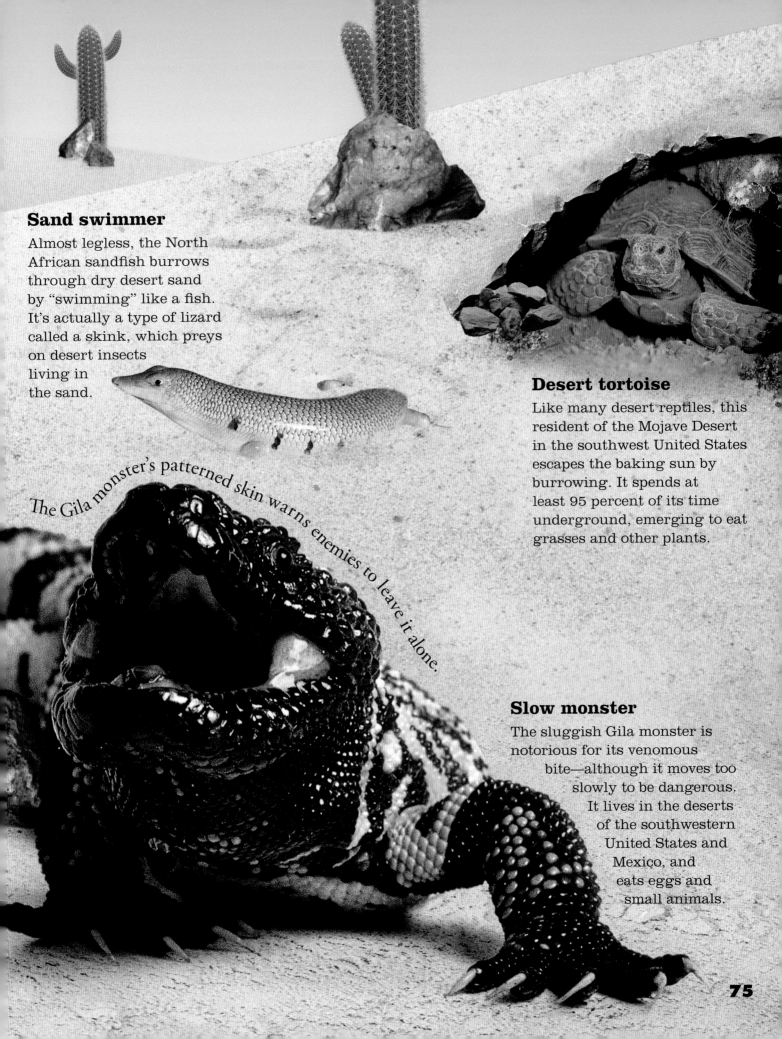

Sand swimmer

Almost legless, the North African sandfish burrows through dry desert sand by "swimming" like a fish. It's actually a type of lizard called a skink, which preys on desert insects living in the sand.

Desert tortoise

Like many desert reptiles, this resident of the Mojave Desert in the southwest United States escapes the baking sun by burrowing. It spends at least 95 percent of its time underground, emerging to eat grasses and other plants.

The Gila monster's patterned skin warns enemies to leave it alone.

Slow monster

The sluggish Gila monster is notorious for its venomous bite—although it moves too slowly to be dangerous. It lives in the deserts of the southwestern United States and Mexico, and eats eggs and small animals.

Ancient **tortoises**

If you think tortoises look ancient, you're right. They've been around since the time of the very first dinosaurs, and have incredibly long life spans. Some have lived for nearly two hundred years—that's an awful lot of birthday candles.

Harriet
This Galápagos tortoise was collected in 1835 by the scientist Charles Darwin. She was taken to Australia in 1841, and lived in various zoos until she died in 2006 at about 175 years old. Harriet's favorite food was hibiscus flowers.

BIRTHDAY **175** GIRL

Diego
For many years, this Galápagos tortoise lived in the San Diego Zoo. But in 1977, he was flown home to join 14 other tortoises from his island. Despite being at least 100, Diego has fathered many baby tortoises, helping to save his species.

Tu'i Malila

In 1953, Britain's Queen Elizabeth II was introduced to a very old tortoise living on the Pacific island of Tongatapu. It had been presented to the King of Tonga by Captain James Cook in 1777. Tu'i Malila eventually died in 1965 at the age of 188.

Lonesome George

There used to be 15 different types of giant tortoises on the Galápagos Islands, but many are now extinct. Until recently, Lonesome George was the last surviving Pinta Island tortoise, but he died around the age of 100 in June 2012.

Adwaita

Nobody knows how old this Aldabra giant tortoise was when he died in 2006. But the story is that he was given to the governor of India around 1765. That would make Adwaita at least 250 years old!

Jonathan

After turning 187 years old in 2019, this giant tortoise from the Seychelles in the Indian Ocean could be the oldest animal alive on the planet. He now lives on the Atlantic island of Saint Helena.

GLOSSARY

antibodies chemicals found in the blood that fight infection and toxins.

antivenom a medicine that treats the effects of venomous snakebites.

bacteria microscopic organisms that live all around us, and even inside us. Some cause disease, but others are vital to health.

cartilage tough, rubbery gristle that forms part of an animal's skeleton.

chromatophores pigmented cells that can get bigger or smaller and thereby change the color of an animal's skin.

cold-blooded an animal that relies on external forces (usually the sun) to keep it warm and active.

constrictor a snake that squeezes its prey to death.

crocodilians the group of reptiles that includes all crocodiles, alligators, and their relatives.

digest to break down food into useful nutrients.

digestive juices fluids released by the stomach and intestines to break down food.

electrostatic forces electrical charges that can make things cling together or force them apart.

evolution the process by which living things change over time.

evolve to change gradually.

extinct having completely died out.

fangs specialized teeth that inject or allow venom into a wound.

fibers slender threads.

fossils the remains or traces of any living thing that survive the normal processes of decay, and are often preserved by being turned to stone.

glands organs in the body that produce vital chemicals.

gullet the tube that connects the mouth and stomach.

hatchling a baby animal that has just emerged from its egg.

hemotoxic describes a chemical that breaks down and destroys blood cells.

herbivore an animal that only eats vegetation (plants).

hibernate to go into a special kind of deep sleep that lasts all winter.

immune not affected by something such as a poison, toxin, or venom.

infrared light emitted by anything radiating warmth, invisible to our eyes.

live bearer an animal that gives birth to babies, rather than laying eggs.

mammal a warm-blooded, usually furry animal that feeds its newborn young on milk.

microscopic too small to be seen without a microscope.

migrating making a regular journey from one region to another, usually due to seasonal temperatures or food resources.

myotoxic describes a venom or poison that attacks the muscles.

neurotoxic describes a venom or poison that attacks the nervous system.

nutrients substances in food that the body needs to build its tissues or provide energy.

paralyze to lose the ability to use muscles that power the movement of body parts such as the limbs or heart.

pit viper a type of viper equipped with heat detectors between the eye and nostril for targeting warm-bodied prey.

predator an animal that hunts and kills other animals for food.

prey an animal that is eaten by another animal.

pupil the dark opening in the eye that lets in light.

quadrate bone bone that links a snake's jaw to its skull.

saliva juices in the mouth that moisten food.

sensor a structure that detects things.

sidewinder a snake that moves by wriggling sideways.

species a population of living organisms that can breed among themselves.

symptoms effects of an illness or injury.

toxic poisonous.

toxin poison.

trachea the breathing tube that brings air to the lungs.

ultraviolet a deep violet light or color that we cannot see, but some other animals can.

venom the chemical that a biting or stinging animal uses for hunting or defense.

venom canal the hollow part of a tooth (fang) used for injecting venom, through which the venom flows.

venomous describes an animal that uses venom for hunting or defense.

vertebrae the bones that, linked together in a chain, form an animal's spine or backbone.

warm-blooded refers to an animal that converts food energy into heat to keep itself warm.

INDEX

CREDITS

The publisher would like to thank the following people for their assistance in the preparation of this book: Daniel Mills for editorial assistance; Taiyaba Khatoon, Sakshi Saluja, and Susie Peachey for picture research; Andrew Kerr, Katie Knutton, and Steve Willis for illustrations; Scarlett O'Hara for proofreading; Chris Bernstein for compiling the index.

Smithsonian Enterprises:
Carol LeBlanc, Vice President
Brigid Ferraro, Director of Licensing
Ellen Nanney, Licensing Manager
Kealy Wilson, Product Development Coordinator